WALKS WITH CHILDREN
IN THE
LAKE DISTRICT

AMBLESIDE AND GRASMERE

Other QUESTA guides

Walks with Children
in the Lake District

AMBLESIDE and
GRASMERE

Dennis and Jan Kelsall

^AQUESTAGuide

ISBN 1 898808 01 5

ADVICE TO READERS

Readers are advised that while the author had made
every effort to ensure the accuracy of this
guidebook, changes can occur which may affect the
contents. The Publishers would welcome notes of any
changes you find.

Maps:
The maps accompanying the walks in this book are
purely diagrammatic, and have been based on maps
produced by (and with the permission of)
Harvey Maps.
© Harvey Maps 1998-2004

Also by Dennis and Jan Kelsall

Walks with Children in the Lake District
South Lakeland
Around Kendal
Around Windermere

Short Walks in the Eden Valley and North Pennines

Published by
Questa Publishing, 27 Camwood, Bamber Bridge, Preston,
Lancashire PR5 8LA
and printed by
Carnmor Print, 95/97 London Road, Preston,
Lancashire PR1 4BA

CONTENTS

INTRODUCTION

Grasmere and Ambleside lie in the picturesque Rothay valley, whose intimate beauty is enhanced by the backdrop of hills, ridges and peaks that rise around it. Running deep into the heart of the rugged mountains, the valley became a convenient route for travellers and traders moving between the more hospitable lowland areas to the north and south. Its history can demonstrate both strategic and economic importance, but more lately can lay claim to being the birthplace of Lakeland tourism.

An unwitting participant in the conception was William Wordsworth, who settled in the area in 1799. The countryside became an inspiration for much of his work, and he quickly emerged as a successful and popular poet. His vivid images of the area excited the imagination of a romantic public, and they in turn arrived to experience the atmosphere for themselves. Wordsworth, as with many subsequent disciples of the area who sometimes feel an exclusive right to its enjoyment, was less than enthusiastic about the visitors, and indeed led opposition against bringing a railway to Windermere, fearing that the unspoilt beauty he so valued would disappear for ever.

Quick, cheap and convenient travel immediately made the Lakes accessible to ordinary people and also brought the first 'commuters', Victorian industrialists who built grand country homes set in wooded gardens around the lakes. Increasing personal mobility, wealth and growing interest in outdoor activity have accelerated the never ending process of change and development, but despite this, the area retains its warranted reputation as one of this country's most enchanting retreats.

Although not exhaustive of all the possible walks in the area, this book will serve to guide you in exploring this beautiful hub of Lakeland from which mountain ranges, lakes and valleys radiate in all directions. Those chosen lead you through the immense diver-

sity and contrast which are contained within these few square kilometres, and hopefully will inspire your imagination in picturing some of its past. Wild open hills, wooded glades, leafy lanes and timeless hamlets are all here to be savoured, and an observant eye will be able to identify some of the traces that history has left.

Some of the walks are justifiably popular, but lose none of their magic or excitement because of it. Regular walkers may be familiar with a route, but the changing seasons and weather create a continually varying environment that gives each day a uniqueness and instills new anticipation. There are quiet corners too, which even on the busiest summer's day, can be almost devoid of people. The views are entrancing, and there is opportunity to experience the sense of ageless remoteness that this small corner of England can create, allowing a complete escape from the urgencies of modern society.

Although the routes are described as walks, we hope that you will do more than that. We have pointed out some things to look for, but there are many more. Watch the backdrop of hills change as your path moves up and down, look in hedgerows and banks, and discover the variety of plants that make up 'grass', turn over stones and look at their colour, compare the buildings that dot the valleys and consider the way in which the workings of the earth, weather, nature and man have combined to create a truly superb landscape.

All the walks are easily accessible from the many car parks provided. The area is also well served by public transport, a bus service runs from the railway station in Windermere and National Express operates a regular coach service directly to Ambleside and Grasmere. Most people will regard these walks, even the shorter ones, as a day's excursion, and each gives opportunities to enjoy a picnic. That does not of course preclude you from visiting one of the many inns or food shops in the area. Be warned, it is almost impossible to walk past the gingerbread shop in Grasmere without being enticed by the heavenly smell emanating from it.

3 Aug 06 — fabulous panora
views, walked ft
the back door of
Holly House Cot

WALK 1
WANSFELL PIKE

Wansfell Pike rises quite abruptly above Ambleside and is a justifiably popular objective. What it lacks in height, it more than makes up for in its strategic position, which, on a fine day, provides one of the best platforms from which to appreciate the long ribbon of Windermere running to the south. All the hard work of the walk is completed in the early stages, with a strenuous, but short, final pull to the top. The return is by an undemanding path across the hill's quiet eastern slopes to Troutbeck, from which an easy track skirts Wansfell's southern flanks back to Ambleside.

Start/Finish: Salutation Hotel at Ambleside. GR.377045.
Total distance: 9.75 km (6 miles).
Height gain: 535m (1752 feet).
Difficulty: The climb to the top of Wansfell is quite strenuous, but then the walking is much easier; Clear paths throughout, but care with young children should be exercised on the road sections.

THE WALK

From the centre of Ambleside behind the Salutation Hotel, walk up a quiet lane, signed 'Waterfalls, Stockghyll and Wansfell Pike'. Part way along, a marked path into Stockghyll Park on the left passes the falls before returning to the lane higher up.

The lane continues its climb, levelling off at a cattle-grid. Just beyond, go over metal ladder stile on the right into a field, where a footpath, signed to 'Troutbeck via Wansfell' climbs beside a stream to a ladder stile at the top. Keep ahead through a gap in a wall by a fractured ash tree just beyond, still following the line of the stream. Higher up, the path crosses the stream and, after passing through a break in a wall, zigzags upwards to find the top.

THE WAY BACK

Leave the hill top, walking eastward to a ladder stile over a fence, beyond which, a clear path falls across the open rolling fellside towards Nanny Lane

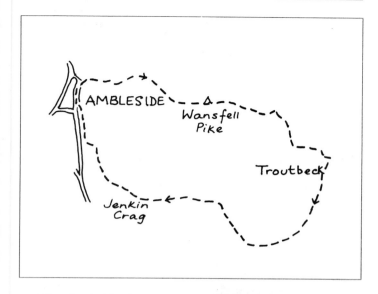

and Troutbeck. You later pass through a wall by a gate and eventually arrive at a second wall, where another gate opens onto a track, Nanny Lane. Turn right and follow it, crossing a gate/stile part-way down, to its end at Lane Foot Farm and join the Kirkstone road at Troutbeck. Turn right and walk past a number of isolated cottages, shortly reaching the post office and a chapel set back from the road on the right, a Christadelphian Meeting Place. There a track, Robin Lane, leaves on the right to Skelghyll, Jenkin Crag and Ambleside.

After gently climbing, the lane levels to an easy walk. Part way along, a stone monolith stands in a field above the path to the right. Reached over a stile, the short climb is rewarded by a wonderful view across Windermere. Further on, at a fork, bear left and go through a gate, your way confirmed by a signpost to 'Skelghyll and Ambleside via Jenkin Crag'.

Now gradually losing height, the track passes through another gate to a stream, beyond which, yet another gate leads to a tarmac drive. Follow it to the right towards High Skelghyll, ignoring a path on the left, and pass the farmhouse through a succession of gates. Beyond, a stone track leads into Skelghyll Wood, later passing a gap in the wall on the left, where a signed path leads a short distance through the trees to emerge on top of Jenkin Crag.

Rejoin the main track through the wood, branching right at a fork, the track beyond shortly zigzagging down to a bridge. Cross over and turn left. Now, stay with the main track, which eventually emerges from the wood and becomes a drive serving the large houses lying hidden in the trees to the right. It finally ends at Old Lake Lane, where you turn right to return to the centre of Ambleside.

ALONG THE WAY
The Salutation Hotel
There has been an inn here for a long time, but it was apparently not always as inviting as it now appears. In 1769, the poet Thomas Gray arrived in Ambleside from Keswick on his way to Kendal, hoping for a bed for the night. He records that he was shown to his room, '..but on looking into the best bed-chamber, dark and damp as a cellar, (I) grew delicate, gave up Wynandermere in despair, and resolved I would go to Kendal directly'.

Stockghyll Force
The waterfalls hidden in the trees provide a dramatic final stage in Stock Ghyll's journey from the hills above to join the River Rothay. They are particularly spectacular after heavy rain, when their foaming waters surge over the rocks and boulders in an unceasing roar. The spot was a great favourite with the Victorian tourists and one can imagine the care with which ladies and young girls, in their voluminous flowing dresses and dainty shoes, would have had to take in walking up to the viewing station.

Ash Trees
The ash, a member of the olive family, is easily recognised in early spring by its distinctive black buds. Many of them in the area have been pollarded, which allowed a regular harvest of useful timber from the crown of the tree whilst leaving the mature trunk intact. The wood is both strong and pliant and was often used to build the frames of horse-drawn wagons.

The Top
During the climb, there is every

justification to pause and admire the panorama sweeping from the north, where a rugged mountainous skyline surrounding the Kirkstone Pass contrasts with the more gentle fells behind you. The summit's relative isolation gives views in all directions. On a clear day, there is a magnificent scene along Windermere to Morecambe Bay in the distance. There are several admirable spots for a picnic around the summit, although as there is still a good walk ahead of you, you might like to wait a little while.

Troutbeck and Town End

As you walk past the ancient cottages that line the road, some of them over four-hundred years old, notice the fine round chimneys that rise above their slated roofs. Also keep your eyes open to observe a number of stone water troughs set into the walls beside the road. In the days before the car, they provided water to refresh the teams of horses that pulled coaches and wagons up the long and arduous climb over the Kirkstone Pass into Patterdale. Each well is adorned with the name of a saint, and no doubt each coachman had his own patron to whom he looked for a safe crossing of the mountains.

Town End, lying a little further along the road beyond Robin Lane, is a well-preserved and homely 17th-century house, typical of those built for well-to-do Lakeland farmers. More recently, it was the home of the Browne family who passed it to the National Trust in 1943.

The interior is furnished with the furniture they collected and gives some idea of the lifestyle that its former inhabitants might have enjoyed. It is advisable to check opening times in advance.

Jenkin Crag

Only a few metres from the path, the rocky outcrop breaking from the trees provides a fine panorama over the northern end of the lake. It is perhaps best enjoyed during the evening of a fine summer's day, when a wonderful stillness accompanies the gently fading light.

WALK 2
DOVE CRAG
and the SCANDALE VALLEY

Dove Crag lies north of Ambleside at the end of the ridge that forms the eastern section of the Fairfield Horseshoe. Our walk, although less ambitious than the Horseshoe, is no less rewarding. Mounting the ascending ridge over Low Pike and then High Pike, a good path then leads easily to Dove Crag. This grand walk makes its return along the Scandale Valley, a quiet place between towering slopes, where sheep and birds are often the only company on a summer's afternoon.

Start/Finish: Junction of Kirkstone Road with the A591 at the north of Ambleside. GR.376047.
Total distance: 14 km (8¾ miles).
Height gain: 740m (2430 feet).
Difficulty: A longer strenuous walk that climbs steadily over the first half. Although in clear weather there are no navigational difficulties, care needs to be taken in mist.

THE WALK

Head north from Ambleside along the main (A591) road towards Rydal and Grasmere. Before the car park on the edge of town, take a narrow road on the right towards Kirkstone and, almost immediately, turn left into Nook Lane. Signed to Low Sweden Bridge, it climbs gently past some satellite buildings of the Charlotte Maison College to end at Nook End Farm.

Walk through the farmyard beyond the buildings to a gate, where a way-marked path bends left to cross Scandale Beck at Low Sweden Bridge. Follow the stream a short distance and then turn sharp right to begin the ascent of the ridge that separates the Rydal and Scandale valleys.

At first, the track climbs above the steep and wooded valley of the stream, but eventually leaves it for the open fellside. A clear track passes through a succession of gateways and accompanying ladder stiles,

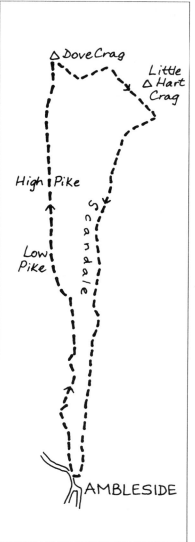

later crossing a broken wall. Beyond, the path carries on ahead and then bends to the left, avoiding some crags to rise behind them towards a wall. The onward route now generally follows this wall to the top of Dove Crag. Paths run on both sides of the wall, and although occasionally the going is easier on the left, the clearer path is usually on the right (eastern) side.

Ahead, the path climbs a succession of terraces to Low Pike and then less steeply, carries on to High Pike. A short final pull brings you to a cairn at its crest. Although the slopes are craggy in places, the route avoids any difficult places and throughout is a good and clear path. Beyond High Pike, the gradient lessens and the going is easier, the clear path still following the wall towards Dove Crag, which is now in view directly ahead. At a small pile of stones, ignore a path to the right which leads to a stark monolithic cairn standing on High Bakestones to the right of the Dove Crag.

Shortly before reaching the summit, by another

13

small cairn, the path crosses the remains of an old fence leaving the wall to the right. Now little more than intermittent iron and wooden posts standing above the tussocky grass of the moor, it marks the line down to Bakestones Moss and can serve as a guide in misty conditions. For the moment, however, continue on to the top of Dove Crag, now only some 350m/yds further on. Its summit cairn lies a little to the right of the path.

THE WAY BACK

From the summit, strike off down the slope to join the dilapidated fenceline passed on the way up. Take care not lose too much height until you reach it, as the ground falls away quite steeply to the left, drawing the unwary onto crags below its eastern flank. Follow the fenceline down to Bakestones Moss. Children should take care as the slope is sometimes quite steep and odd lengths of rusting wire lie hidden by the grass.

Later, the path levels across the moss, which can be quite wet in places. Keep following the fence, it eventually turns to the right and then later crosses the middle of a small shallow grassy tarn, a line of stones providing convenient steps to allow you to cross with dry feet. Beyond the tarn, at a gentle bend in the fence, a trod on the left winds a short distance between small pools towards an outcrop of rock, Little Hart Crag. Even though of modest height, the crag achieves prominence by virtue of its relative isolation and splendid views reward the short detour to its two tops, the lower one lying about 100m/yds further on.

Return to the fence and continue following it downwards, eventually reaching a wall by a hollow containing a small pool. Follow it left to a corner and then round to the right, dropping to a ladder stile at the head of Scandale Pass. The route to Ambleside lies over the wall, the path dropping into Scandale along a tongue of ground separating two of the three main streams that combine lower down to produce Scandale Beck.

After passing through an open gateway by a stone-walled sheepfold, the path becomes a wide and substantial track, shortly crossing a brook.

Beyond, the track rises gently through another gate over the top of a knoll, where an enclosure rising up the hillside on the left is sparsely populated with Scots pines. Further down, after moving to the right to avoid low hillocks of glacial deposit, the stream is again brought close to the path by the narrowing valley, the two eventually meeting at High Sweden Bridge whose graceful stone arch is a fine example of Lakeland craftsmanship.

Remain on the left bank, following the track through a couple of gates to its end, where a final gate leads onto Sweden Bridge Lane. Walk down to its junction with Kirkstone Road, and turn right to return to the town.

ALONG THE WAY
Leaving Ambleside
As you climb, notice a house on the left, whose date of construction is shown as 1661. Charles II was then on the throne, the monarchy having just been restored after the Civil Wars. Such details serve remind us of the antiquity of settlement in these valleys.

Low Sweden Bridge
Before the advent of the turnpike roads, travel through the lakes was slow and arduous and goods (and people) travelled on the backs of ponies and horses along the old 'packhorse' trails. Many rivers and streams were forded, but in some places, as here at Low Sweden Bridge, sturdy practical bridges were built to carry the road above an otherwise dangerous crossing. It is a fine example of a packhorse bridge, a delicate and pleasing single stone arch that belies its serviceability. A second one is passed higher up the stream on the second part of the walk.

High Pike
From High Pike, its summit marked by a cairn, there is an impressive all-round panorama of the surrounding mountains. To the south, beyond Windermere and Coniston is Morecambe Bay and, on a good day, Blackpool Tower might be spotted. To the south-east the view is open to the Pennines and the crisp, clear days of autumn and winter are often the best times to appreciate the scene. This is a good spot to spend a little time with your map and compass, identifying the neighbouring peaks, not only to know their names, but to gain experience in using these indispensable companions of the walker.

WALK 3
AN AMBLESIDE AMBLE

*Squeezed as it is between the steeply rising hills of Loughrigg to the
west and Wansfell to the east, Ambleside gives little opportunity for a
gentle stroll around its edge without necessitating a climb onto the
surrounding steep hills. However, the Rothay valley, immediately
to the north, provides a useful alternative for a peaceful and
undemanding circular walk for those not wishing to venture
too far afield.*

Start/Finish: Car park, Ambleside. GR.376047.
Total distance: 6.75km (4¼ miles).
Height gain: Negligible.
Difficulty: An undemanding walk; take care on the sections along the
main road.

THE WALK

Begin along the main (A591)
road, heading north towards
Grasmere. Just outside the
town, after crossing Scandale
Beck, fork right through a pair of
iron gates onto a drive that leads
through parkland to Rydal Hall.
Just before reaching the Hall,
the waymarked track turns to
the right, crosses Rydal Beck
above the Lower Falls and
passes around the back of the
Hall where there are some barns
and a tea shop. Continue past
the Hall to emerge onto a lane
by Rydal Mount.

OPTIONAL EXTENSION TO RYDAL FALLS

Emerging from Rydal Hall onto
the lane, turn right and walk up
past Rydal Mount to a gate.
Ignore the track on the left to
Grasmere, but go ahead, passing in front of a farm house and
choose the right fork signed
'Access Area'.

Walk on a short distance to
another gate, there going right
through a kissing-gate in the
wall, signed 'Birk Hagg and
Rydal Falls'. A woodland path
leads to a gate and then drops
to a foot-bridge across Rydal
Beck. On the far bank, turn left
and follow a climbing path be-

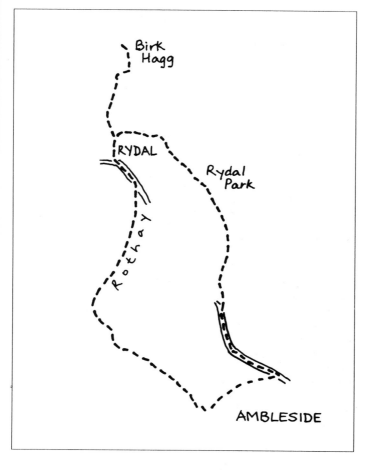

side the stream. Although not particularly high, the falls are quite spectacular, the head of the largest drop being blocked by a fallen boulder, under which the water gushes.

Retrace your steps past Rydal Mount.

THE WAY BACK

Walk down the lane to the main road. Turn left, and cross over,

17

taking particular care with children and dogs as it can be very busy.

After only a short distance, turn right into a quiet lane. Cross Pelter Bridge and, bearing left at the junction, follow the road for about 1.75km (1 mile) until you come to a bridge over the river on the left. Across the bridge, keep walking ahead on a footpath, eventually coming to a street. Go to the main road its far end and turn right into Ambleside town centre.

ALONG THE WAY
Ambleside
Occupying an important place at the cross-roads of the natural east-west and north-south routes through central Lakeland, Ambleside has probably always been a busy spot.

Recorded history of the town began with the arrival of the Romans, who established a settlement beside the road they built to the coast at Ravenglass (Glanoventa).

Later came the Vikings, whose presence is remembered in the many place-names derived from their language; beck, pike, tarn, ghyll are some examples. Indeed, the name Ambleside possibly derived from Amal's Saeter, or farmstead.

In medieval times, a thriving village grew up alongside the packhorse route to the north and it was granted market charters in 1650 and 1688. The remains of the old market cross from those days still stand in front of the Salutation hotel.

Rydal Falls
Rydal Falls were a notable attraction for Victorian tourists, and such was their fame that they became one of the most painted subjects in the area. They now seem to have been largely forgotten, partly because the Lower Falls lie close to the Hall, to which for some time there was no public access. These lie just downstream from the barns, the small stone building on the bank below them was erected so that artists could continue painting during rain. A small detour is necessary to see the Upper Falls but the effort is well rewarded.

WALK 4
LOUGHRIGG TARN

*Loughrigg Tarn is one of Lakeland's many delights, a beautiful pool of
water in an idyllic setting, surrounded by sloping pastures and
nestling at the foot of Loughrigg Fell. Although readily accessible, it
retains a detachment from the bustle of everyday life. This walk to it
from Rothay Park in Ambleside follows a roughly circular route over
the lower southern slopes of Loughrigg Fell.*

Start/Finish: Rothay Park, Ambleside. GR.374043.
Total distance: 7.5km (4¾ miles).
Height gain: 290m (950 feet).
Difficulty: An easy walk, involving only a modest climb.

THE WALK

Rothay Park lies to the north-
west of the town behind St
Mary's Church and is signed
from the main road. Walk
through the park to its north-
western corner, where a path
leaves across Miller Bridge onto
a lane. Turn right and after some
50m/yds, turn left across a cattle grid and go up a drive climbing to Brow Head Farm.

As it passes the farm, the
drive first bends sharply left and
then right. At that point leave it
over a stile on the left for a
marked footpath around the
edge of Miller Brow Wood. At
the end, cross a squeeze stile
and stream and follow a

waymarked trod climbing to the
right up a bracken covered hillside. In a few m/yds, where it
splits, take the left fork and carry
on to a wall. Cross it and walk
ahead to a rocky outcrop from
which there is a dramatic view
along Windermere. In a field
below at the head of the lake,
you can see the outline of
Ambleside's Roman fort.

The path now turns right to a
ladder stile over a stone wall.
Go right on a path that initially
runs beside it then heads out
across the undulating fell. Keep
ahead, shortly picking as an
objective, a lone tree, but just
before reaching it, turn right on
a gently climbing path. After

passing to the right of a small tarn, go on over a crest to Lily Tarn. Pass that also on the right and, ignoring crossing tracks, follow an undulating path that generally follows the line of a wall lying over to the left. After passing through a gate in a wire fence, you will eventually cross a small stream, climbing the bank on the far side to a junction of paths near Ivy Crag.

[For those climbing to the top of Loughrigg Fell, the way now lies ahead, continue with the directions given in Walk 5.]

For Loughrigg Tarn, turn left along a clear descending track below Ivy Crag. Take either fork where it splits lower down, but that on the right gives the better view beyond Elter Water into Great Langdale.

After passing through a gate, the way drops through a wooded area of larch, beech, oak and Scots pine and becomes enclosed by walls and shortly bends to the left. Just beyond, take a waymarked track through the second of two adjacent gates on the right.

Walk ahead by the edge of a field to a stile and keep going to a second one that leads onto a drive. Across to the right, a final stile gives access to the meadows that surround Loughrigg Tarn, the sloping banks providing an ideal picnic spot.

THE WAY BACK

The first part of the return route retraces the outward journey onto the fell by Ivy Crag.

To remind you, climb back to the drive and cross over the opposite stile. Walk across two meadows to a gate through which, turn left and follow the track uphill, eventually reaching the stream, the path naturally leading you to cross it a few m/yds upstream from the point you first crossed.

Once over, walk on ahead, shortly arriving at gate in a stone wall by a stand of larch trees. Walk through and keep going, the path dropping gently.

After passing a solitary oak you later reach another a stone wall, where a sign directs you right, alongside it, towards Ambleside. After losing more height, go through a gate and walk past Pine Rigg, a house over to the left.

The path, now a stony track, falls to another gate and stile and, eventually, rejoins the outward route at Brow Head Farm.

Keep on to the end of the track and turn right to Miller Bridge and Rothay Park.

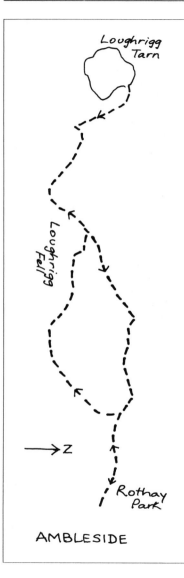

ANOTHER WAY BACK

An alternative return is by way of Red Bank, Loughrigg Terrace and Rydal. Although longer, there is less climbing and, in passing both Grasmere and Rydal Water, there is a further opportunity to enjoy lake scenery.

Climb back to the drive, but instead, turn left, walking to the road at its end. Turn right and walk up to Red Bank. At the crest of the hill, just past a junction with the Elterwater road, leave by a gated track on the right which leads into Deer Bolts Wood and to the path across Loughrigg Terrace.

Follow the route given in Walk 9 from there to Pelter Bridge. Turn right and follow the lane beside the Rothay back to Miller Bridge.

ALONG THE WAY
Galava Fort

When the Romans arrived in the first century AD, they found the head of Windermere ideally placed to supervise the several valleys that converge on the head of the lake. They consolidated their presence by building a wooden fort in about 79 AD and went on to build a remarkable mountain road across the Wrynose and Hardknott Passes to reach the coast at Ravenglass.

About forty years later, they replaced the wooden structure with stone buildings, the low remains of which lie in a meadow beside the Rothay where it meets the lake. The site was excavated before the Second World War and is now cared for by the National Trust. It can be visited from the town.

Loughrigg Fell

Loughrigg Fell (meaning 'Ridge above the Lake) is criss-crossed by any number of paths that meander between rocky outcrops and grassy hillocks.

On a good day, it is an ideal place to explore. There is little danger of getting seriously lost, providing a general sense of direction and position are maintained. Your map and compass are, of course, invaluable tools and this is a good place to spend a profitable afternoon improving your skill in their use.

Rothay Park

Rothay Park was established as a public recreation ground by the local council in 1902, when three fields known as Jimmy Jackson Field or Cragg Ing, White Flatt and Miller Field were acquired for the purpose.

THE NATIONAL TRUST

If asked, many people will identify the National Trust with stately homes and formal gardens, and forget the tremendous amount of care and effort that is directed towards maintaining different aspects of the countryside. In Lakeland, the Trust looks after more than a quarter of the National Park, managing many diverse land types to preserve natural beauty, conserve wildlife habitats, promote traditional farming practices and, of course, create access. As you walk, look out for the distinctive signs that indicate the land owned by the Trust. And, if you are not already a member of the Trust, do consider joining; there are many benefits to be had.

WALK 5
LOUGHRIGG FELL
from Ambleside

Although the height gain is about the same, the ascent of Loughrigg from Ambleside is a more gentle climb than that which rises from the shores of Grasmere (Walk 8). Whilst some might regard this as justification for considering it a preferred route, it should be viewed rather as an opportunity to explore the varied topography and fine views of this much-loved fell.

Start/Finish: Rothay Park, Ambleside. GR.374043.
Total distance: 7km (4¼ miles), or 9.5km (6 miles) for the longer walk.
Height gain: 330m (1080 feet).
Difficulty: The easiest ascent of Loughrigg, the climb being steady; pay attention to navigation in mist.

THE WALK

Follow the instructions in Walk 4 (Loughrigg Tarn) to reach the stream below Ivy Crag.

After crossing it, walk ahead on a climbing track, ignoring any crossing paths. It levels, first to pass a rocky outcrop and then again at a rather wet area, dotted with tiny tarns.

Keep ahead to a junction and take a level path to the left which soon widens to a broad grass track. After dropping to cross a depression, it again climbs and the top of Loughrigg can now be seen ahead. The way, no longer in doubt, is marked by occasional large cairns, but the trig point on the summit remains hidden almost until the last moment, when a dramatic view northward along Dunmail Raise is revealed.

THE WAY BACK

The most obvious return is to retrace your outward route and in so doing, enjoy the open views to the south that you might have not fully appreciated on the way up.

As an alternative, you might continue walking over the summit to follow a path that descends to the western end of

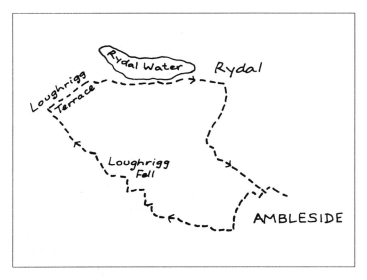

Loughrigg Terrace. From there, follow the directions to Rydal given in Walk 9 as far as Pelter Bridge and then return to Ambleside along the lane beside the River Rothay as indicated in Walk 3.

BLUEBELLS

Early in the year, Loughrigg's flanks above Rydal Water are washed in a delicate shade of blue, which on closer inspection, resolves into a mass of bluebells. These delightful plants, which are heralds of spring, are more commonly found carpeting deciduous woods, eager to produce their flowers before the emerging canopy of leaves steals the sun's rays. Their strategy is the same here, for as summer comes, the hillsides become enveloped in bracken, whose dense foliage prevents even grass retaining a secure foothold.

WALK 6
ELTER WATER
and LITTLE LANGDALE

*Although not strictly within the geographical confines set by the title
of this book, the attractive setting of Elter Water is revealed during the
walk to Loughrigg Tarn and its appeal is just too much to ignore.
Starting from the small hamlet of Elterwater, this is a delightful low-
level walk, though not without occasional short pulls. Its varied terrain
illustrates many aspects of lakeland topography, beginning in a wide,
flat valley surrounded by steeply rising fells. In winter, the low-lying
riverside meadows can flood and occasionally make parts of the early
section of this walk quite wet. There are several stretches that pass
through mixed deciduous woodland, and the walk also wanders onto
the fringes of the wilder fellside, giving a taste of the remoteness that
their openness can generate.*

Start/Finish: Elterwater village. GR.327047.
Total distance: 9km (5½ miles).
Height gain: 180m (590 feet).
Difficulty: There is no particular difficulty, but exercise care with young
children near streams.

THE WALK

Leave the car park by a kissing gate at its far end and follow a riverside path to Skelwith Bridge. Largely hidden by trees, Elter Water (Norse for Lake of the Swans) can be glimpsed ahead, but before reaching it, the path moves away around a woodland fringe.

Shortly, steepening ground forces the path back to the water and you enter a meadow at the far end of the lake. Walk ahead, passing through a gate in the middle, along a well used and obvious path, that can become wet after rain. Once through a field-gate at the far end, the path again follows the stream. The valley, now wooded, narrows, forcing the stream to tumble over great boulders on its way to Skelwith Force. The winter cascades are said to be the largest in the area

25

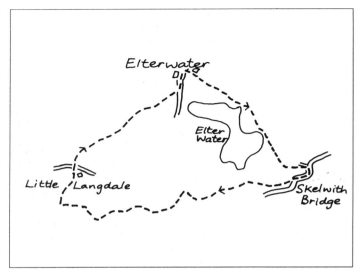

in terms of water volume. If you clamber down for a closer look at the water, take care. The path shortly leads you through the stone yard of Kirkstone Quarries and out onto the road at Skelwith Bridge.

Over the bridge, take the right fork and after about 100m/yds, leave the road by a footpath on the right into Bridge How Coppice and climb an oak and beech clad bank to a gate into a pasture beyond.

Follow a gravel drive to the right, shortly coming to a house.

There is now a better view of Elterwater and, beyond, in Great Langdale, there is as good a sight as any of Pavey Ark and

Harrison Stickle, standing sentinel over the valley.

The track passes left of the house, passing some caravans on its way to Park Farm. As you walk through the farmyard, look for a stone tablet in the wall of the last barn on the left. On it are neatly carved six alphabets, five of them in upper case. It is an exhibition piece, produced by a stonemason to demonstrate his skill.

Just beyond, go to the right between some outbuildings and follow a track that gently falls to a stile and then on to another farm. Walk on through a kissing-gate into a meadow and cross to a stile, over which the path drops down a steeply wooded bank. After then passing through another small meadow, the path ends at a final stile at a lane.

Turn right and then cross another stile, just along on the left. The path forking right climbs upstream by a river, gaining height above its steeply wooded banks, to give a fine vantage of Colwith Force.

More dramatic than those at Skelwith, Colwith Force cascades over a low cliff and is split by an outcropping rock to produce a double plume falling into a deep, dark pool below.

Above the falls, the path briefly follows the river before turning back into the woods, eventually meeting a track from the left at a field-gate.

Go through, turn right and follow the meadow wall to another gate. Through this, walk across towards the cottage at High Park, leaving the field by a final gate.

Turn left up to a track and then go right to Stang End. There, go ahead between the cottages and barns and then bend left over a cattle grid to Hallgarth and Tilberthwaite. The track drops through open woodland, crossing a stream and eventually meeting the river. Follow it upstream past the now disused Hallgarth Quarries on the left. A little further on, beyond a gate, go through a wicket to a bridge across the river, Slater Bridge. It was built by the quarrymen who utilised a well constructed arch, a convenient boulder and a simple clapper bridge to carry a path across the water.

On the other bank, climb a path by a wall, signposted to Elterwater, and which leads to High Birk Howe Farm. Carry on to the lane beyond. There turn left and then immediately go right, gently climbing to Dale End Farm. Beyond, the way deteriorates to a stone track, climbing to a low saddle before dropping down into Langdale. Take the right junction each time it forks and you will eventually reach the Elterwater road. Turn left along it and walk the short distance back into the village.

ALONG THE WAY

Upstream from Skelwith Force, the water was used to power a bobbin mill, one of many that contributed to a thriving local industry. In the surrounding area, birch and hazel trees were coppiced, the slender boughs then being cut and turned to produce bobbins to supply the expanding cotton industries of Yorkshire and Lancashire.

WALK 7
ALCOCK TARN

Alcock Tarn lies cradled in a shallow fold, high on the eastern flank of Heron Pike above Grasmere. Although only a short excursion, it gives the walker a true taste of the rugged open fellsides. The return route, at first, drops quite steeply for a short stretch and may require a little care for those with very young children. However, this can be avoided by returning along the outward route, along which the gradient is less demanding. At all times, the paths are well defined and present no navigational problems to the walker.

Start/Finish: White Moss car park. GR.348065.
Total distance: 6km (3¾ miles).
Height gain: 420m (1375 feet).
Difficulty: After a steady climb to the tarn, the first part of the descent is quite steep and requires care.

THE WALK

Begin along a gravel track that leaves the main (A591) road, immediately east of the car park on the northern side of the road at White Moss. It climbs beside White Moss Common to a narrow lane at the top. There, again turn left and walk past a small pond surrounded by trees on the right.

A little further on, just before the lane bends down to the left, bear right along a gravel track, climbing gently into woodland and signed 'Alcock Tarn'. The track later levels and narrows between enclosing walls. Ignore

the path to the right and walk ahead through a gate into woodland. A clear track gently climbs, passing through another gate to a fork. You will return along the left-hand path coming back, but for the moment, take the right branch. The path continues climbing, shortly leaving the trees to zigzag up the hillside.

Beyond an iron gate, the climb continues, passing through a broken gap in a stone wall and, later, crossing a stream emanating from Alcock Tarn, still hidden above. After that, the path climbs more steeply to Grey Crag, a prominent out-

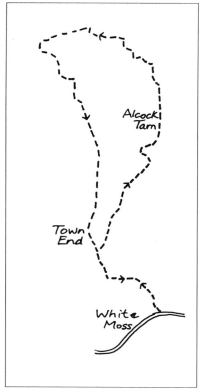

THE WAY BACK

Follow a path on the left bank of the tarn, crossing a stile in a wall at the far end. The path avoids a marshy area, draining into Greenhead Gill, and comes to a large cairn. Ahead, across the deep valley, is Stone Arthur and to the right rise Heron Pike and Great Rigg.

The path now drops steeply and a little care is needed on the zigzags down the incline. Although rocky at the top, it soon become grassy and, as the gradient eases, the path heads towards the far corner of a wall enclosing a small plantation, where it meets a track from Heron Pike. Turn left, the way now much easier along the valley.

Shortly the path joins the banks of the gill, continuing beside it until forced across a wooden bridge by a wall. Once across, go through a gate and walk down the lane.

crop rising ahead, where a rocky perch to the right of the path gives a fine view over Grasmere. The remainder of the climb is more gentle, the path eventually leading to gap in a stone wall, beyond which is Alcock Tarn.

At the bottom, turn left and then go left again at the first junction. Walk past some houses and, where the lane bends sharply right, go through a gate on the left into Grasmere Lodge.

Walk ahead, passing just to the right of the building in front, and go through another gate behind it. A short track leads to yet another gate into a wood. Go through and turning right to follow the wall. Eventually, the path rises to a stile and then, after a level stretch, climbs up to the left, shortly arriving at a small clearing.

Bear right to find another stile, the path beyond shortly crossing a stream by a narrow bridge. Keep going, roughly parallel to a wall over to the right, you will eventually pass through a kissing gate, after which the path rises to a junction, rejoining the route of your outward journey. Turn right and retrace your steps to the car park.

ALONG THE WAY
Alcock Tarn

The grassy banks surrounding Alcock Tarn provide ideal spots to enjoy a picnic, but take care with small children at the water's edge. The tarn is a small reservoir, retained by a low dam. As you explore the area around it, you will discover that, if the holding wall had been much higher, the outflow would, in fact, have been in the opposite direction, its waters adding to the trickle that already finds its way into Greenhead Gill.

In tumbling down its deep valley, the waters of Greenhead Gill have created some waterfalls. Near there, notice on the far bank, just above the stream, a hole into the hillside. This is an adit, the entrance to old mine workings. These hills around Grasmere were once mined for lead and iron ore. The low humps that dot the surrounding hillsides are piles of spoil from the mining activity. The bridge which crosses the stream carries a water pipeline.

This corner of Lakeland, above Rydal, was a particular favourite of the Wordsworths, and they spent many hours wandering through the woods and open fells. Greenhead Gill, into which Walk 7 leads you, is evocatively described in his poem 'Michael':

...The mountains have all opened out themselves, And made a hidden valley of their own...

WALK 8
LOUGHRIGG FELL
from White Moss

Despite its diminutive size, Loughrigg is perhaps as well known to Lakeland visitors as Helvellyn or even Scafell Pike. Its popularity derives from its accessibility and the relative ease with which its top can be reached. Well positioned with regard to the surrounding high ground, it offers impressive views in all directions from its summit, which give a distinct sense of achievement from the climb. There are several paths up, this being the shortest and therefore the steepest. However, all the climbing is tackled early in the walk and you are rewarded with a fine and easy return walk on which to enjoy incomparable views over the lakes.

Start/Finish: Rydal Water car park. GR.350064.
Total distance: 8.5km (5¼ miles).
Height gain: 325m (1064 feet).
Difficulty: A demanding climb to the top, but then an easier walk. Not really suitable for misty conditions without navigation skills.

THE WALK

A woodland track from the far end of the car park leads to the River Rothay, following it upstream to a bridge. Cross over and walk away along a path signed 'Loughrigg Terrace'. It climbs through trees to a stone wall and gate onto the open fell. Through the gate, turn right and then almost immediately, at a fork, go left on a gradually rising path across Loughrigg Terrace to the top corner of an enclosed wood ahead. Just before the wall, turn sharp left onto a path which rises steeply up the hillside.

Higher up, at a cairn, a moment's pause allows an opportunity to admire the view. Keep going to a steep grass slope, the path there being waymarked to avoid the direct ascent by climbing more gently to the left for a short distance. The path then curves right and after a short pull, levels to a hillocky plateau. The summit lies a little further on, the path leading directly to a trig point.

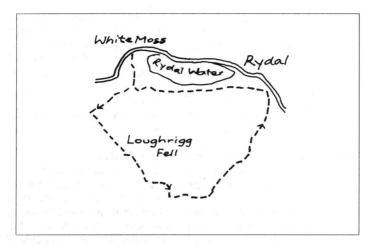

THE WAY BACK

Maintain your original direction and continue over the summit, dropping to a cairn from which a clear grass path leads on ahead. Follow it into a small gully, the way being clear and occasionally cairned. As it undulates downwards across grass and bracken covered slopes, sometimes winding to avoid outcrops of rock, there are engaging views ahead and to the right across to Elter Water.

After a while the path comes close to a wall on the right, keep going, but just beyond, at a fork, take the right branch and pass by a small grassy hollow accommodating small tarns. Follow the path to the right to bypass a rocky hillock rising before you. The path curves around it and becomes more pronounced as it again descends.

Ignore grass tracks off to the right, and keep ahead, making for a large boggy depression bearing the evocative title 'Black Mire'. A short drop brings you to a small pool, passed on the left, and beyond, a stream crosses the path.

Go over and maintain your direction, crossing another junction of paths. The path then bends left, leading towards a gate by a stand of larch ahead. Before reaching the gate, go left on a path beside a wall, which almost immediately bends right to go downhill.

As you lose height, the hillside becomes wooded and eventually you pass through a mass of rhododendron bushes to cross a stream over a stone slab bridge.

Walk up to a kissing-gate and then pass behind an interestingly-roofed and ' many-chimneyed house, Fox Gill. The path finally ends through a gate at a lane; here turn left and walk towards Pelter Bridge.

At a junction just before Pelter Bridge, go left and walk up to a gate at the end of the lane. Keep going along a woodland track, shortly emerging from the trees above Rydal Water.

Remain with the high path to the far end of the lake, where it meets a path rising from the shore. Go right, now re-tracing your outward path, remembering to go left at the gate to drop through the wood to the river.

ALONG THE WAY

In spite of its relatively insignificant height at only 335 metres, the summit of Loughrigg gives wonderful views in all directions. There is a slightly lower outcrop to the left which gives one of the best scenes over Rydal Water below.

The area surrounding the fell is 'lumpy', and undulates gently downwards to the south-east, culminating at the head of Windermere beside Ambleside. If it is windy, there are ample opportunities for a picnic stop a little further on, where there is more shelter amongst the rocks and grassy hillocks.

Pelter Bridge

Part way along the lane to Pelter Bridge, a signed footpath on the right leads to stepping stones that take the path across the Rothay. The house on the left at this point was the home of Wordsworth's last surviving grandson, Gordon Wordsworth, who died in 1935.

WALK 9
RYDAL WATER

Rydal Water lies at the foot of Nab Scar, the near precipitous southern abutment of Heron Pike that complements the steeply rising slopes of Loughrigg on the opposite bank. It is fed by the River Rothay, which descends Dunmail Raise as Raise Beck and passes through Grasmere before arriving here. The river re-appears at the lake's eastern outflow to complete its journey to Windermere. This short and easy stroll around Rydal Water is ideal for a pleasant evening, but equally worthy of a full day, as there are many spots to enjoy a picnic.

Start/Finish: Rydal Water car park. GR.350064.
Total distance: 5km (3¼ miles).
Height gain: 130m (430 feet).
Difficulty: The walk is undemanding, but take care when crossing the main road.

THE WALK

Take the wide track into trees that runs to the River Rothay, following it upstream to a bridge. Cross over and climb the path ahead to Loughrigg Terrace.

At the top leave the wood, and turn left. After gently losing height towards the lakeshore follow it for a distance. Where the main track later leaves the shore, remain with the lower lakeside path, walking ahead through a gate into more trees. Further on, leave through another gate, returning to the water's edge as the lake narrows and the river again asserts its individuality. Keep going

to a bridge and cross over to the main road by the Glen Rothay Hotel. Exercise care at this point, as the road is often busy.

Turn right and walk along the road for about 100m/yds before then turning left past St Mary's Church to Rydal Mount.

Part way up on the right is the entrance to Rydal Hall, where teas are served during the summer.

Just past Rydal Mount at the top, go left on a bridleway, signposted to 'Grasmere'. After climbing past Hart Head Barn, go through a gate ahead, after which the gradient eases. The track, occasionally walled on

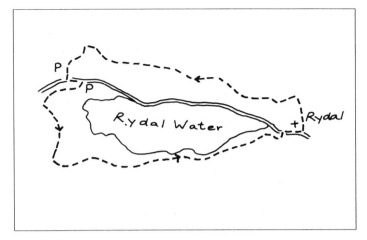

one or both sides, undulates easily below the steep slopes of Nab Scar rising to the right of the path. After some 1.5km (1 mile), and a succession of gates, the path eventually emerges as a gravel drive.

Keep going a short distance, and after crossing a small stream, take a descending path on the left. It follows the stream, passing through a gate part way down, to end at the main road close to the car park.

ALONG THE WAY
Rydal

The names of many places are descriptive of some local feature or association. Two possible meanings have been suggested for Rydal, both deriving from the Norse 'rudh dalr'. One suggests a forest clearing and the other a dale where rye was grown.

Another early name, Routhamere, sprang from the river that passes through it, and describes it as a trout stream. Whatever its origins, these theories all depict aspects of this picturesque lake and lower valley.

Rydal Hall

Rydal Hall was built as the family home of the Flemmings who originated at Coniston Hall, some 12km (7½ miles) to the south-west. The 17th-century building, later 'modernised' with a Victorian facade, replaces an earlier hall that stood further downstream. It is now run by the Carlisle Diocese as a conference and study centre and is not open to the general public.

Rydal Mount

Rydal Mount was William Wordsworth's home from 1813 until his death in 1850. He set out the large gardens, carefully planting the trees so that they framed his beloved picturesque views. Although he never owned property, he bought a small plot of land, now known as Dora's Field, behind St Mary's Church intending to build a house on it. The profuse daffodils which sprout from it in spring are, however, not the ones referred to in his poem. To see these, you must journey to Gowbarrow Park beside Ullswater. Dora's Field is now owned by the National Trust.

St Mary's Church

St Mary's Church, was built in 1824 when Rydal was granted the status of a parish in its own right and was regularly attended by the Wordsworths.

One of the windows is dedicated to Thomas Arnold, headmaster at Rugby school from 1828 until his early death in 1842, at the age of 47. He built the house at nearby Fox How,

intending it for his retirement. Arnold appears as a character in the book 'Tom Brown's Schooldays', written by Thomas Hughes, who was at one-time a pupil of his.

Coffin road

The track from Rydal to Grasmere was once part of the main packhorse route between Ambleside and Keswick. It served as a coffin road, as before St Mary's Church was built at Rydal, the hamlet's dead were taken to Grasmere for burial in the churchyard at St Oswald's.

WALK 10
RYDAL QUARRIES

Above the southern shore of Rydal Water, burrowing into the hillside below Loughrigg, are some massive caves that were excavated as a result of stone quarrying. No longer worked, their empty vastness now holds a fascination, particularly for children, who will almost certainly wish to explore their dark interiors. They are reached by a variation to the previous walk (Walk 9).

Start/Finish: Rydal Water car park. GR.350064.
Total distance: 5km (3¼ miles).
Height gain: 160m (524 feet).
Difficulty: After a short climb, the continuing route is not arduous.

THE WALK

Follow the directions given in Walk 9 as far as the gate from the small wood onto Loughrigg Terrace. Instead of turning left to walk around the lake, go right a short distance to meet a path joining from the left. Turn sharp left onto it and walk at a higher level above the lake, eventually coming to the caves.

Beyond the caves, the path carries on into woodland, eventually terminating at a gate. Go through, shortly passing some cottages on the right.

Now on a descending lane, pass a small car park and walk to a junction by Pelter Bridge. Turn left to cross the river and gain the main road. Again turn left along it (beware of traffic) and after a short distance, turn right to climb past St Mary's Church and follow the return described in Walk 9 to the car park.

ALONG THE WAY

A path leads directly into the gaping mouth of the larger cave beside a large pool of water that almost fills its entrance. The void measures some 50m/yds by 25 and is perhaps 10m/yds high. Wainwright, in his book of the area, suggests that there is room to accommodate the whole population of Ambleside, although he acknowledges that

37

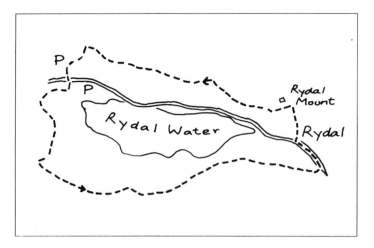

some will have to stand in the water, which continually drips from the roof, adding to the pool. Observant eyes will spot where the drills have cut into the rock during the quarrying operations.

The second cavern is separated from the path by a gully and it requires a little scramble to enter, take care with small children.

SCOTS PINE

The Scots pine, as its name suggests, is native to Britain. However, much of what we now see today in Lakeland has been planted, and is a variety imported from mainland Europe.
The difference between the two species can be discerned in the mature tree, the native strain grows to a pyramid top that becomes rounded with age, whilst the European variety produces a flat-topped crown.

WALK 11
STONE ARTHUR

Stone Arthur rises above Grasmere to the north and is the termination of a subsidiary ridge climbing back over Great Rigg to Fairfield that separates the deep valleys of Great Tongue Gill and Greenhead Gill. The climb up to it is quite steep, the gradient rarely relenting. Yet, despite this, it is an uncomplicated walk along distinct paths and affords an impressive view of the almost canyon-like qualities of Greenhead Gill. For much of the ascent, Stone Arthur deceptively appears as a summit in its own right, but once reached, its relation to the rest of the ridge becomes obvious.

Start/Finish: Grasmere. GR.336076.
Total distance: 5km (3¼ miles).
Height gain: 430m (1408 feet).
Difficulty: Quite tiring; young children will need encouragement.

THE WALK

Walk north-east from Grasmere along Broadgate and Swan Lane to cross the main (A591) road at the Swan Hotel, with care. Go up a lane beside the hotel, taking the second turning on the right into a narrow lane to Greenhead Gill and Alcock Tarn. The lane climbs gently beside the gill, the bright and sparkling waters, collected from the open fells above, dash over lichen and moss covered boulders that separate a succession of shallow pools.

On a hot day, the cooling babble re-enforces the shade provided by the trees enclosing its course.

Go through a gate at the end of the lane and take a path on the left that climbs steeply beside a drystone wall and tree plantation.

Higher up, at the end of the wall, ignore the gap ahead and follow the waymarked path to the right. Before continuing however, pause to enjoy the fine view beyond the gap to Helm Crag, Easedale and Green Burn. The path remains steep, steadily climbing the bracken-cloaked slopes above Greenhead Gill.

Shortly, high up on the left, Stone Arthur, comes into view, its rocky buttress standing sentinel above the deep cleft of the valley. The path obligingly takes a less direct approach, continuing its steady ascent along the valley.

After crossing a small stream, the gradient eases somewhat and eventually you pass a lone sycamore, isolated from any company by an ocean of bracken. It stands in defiance of the elements and offers welcome shade on a hot summer day. Another pull and the path then bends left, becoming an open grass track. It climbs to meet a stone wall, but shortly leaves it to the right, again assuming a steeper gradient as it now climbs directly towards Stone Arthur.

Above, the path winds to seek the easiest line through the craggy bastions. There is no difficulty, but shorter legs may treat it more as an easy scramble than a walk.

It is only at the top of the rocks that the 'summit' loses its apparent independence, the ridge behind, continuing over Great Rigg to Fairfield, now becoming visible. There is thus no specific point to mark the end of the walk, but any number of projecting rocky outcrops will serve as perches from which to enjoy your picnic and the view. They also provide an ideal opportunity for those with energy left to practise their scrambling skills, young children, of course, being supervised.

TO GO FURTHER

On a fine day, the walk may be safely extended to Great Rigg or even on to Fairfield itself, since the steepest part of the ascent has now been made. However, Fairfield is still some 360m (1,200 feet) higher and about 4km (2½ miles) away, a significant additional distance for young legs.

Unless you are an experienced walker, the extension should not be attempted in misty conditions, since the top of Fairfield can be confusing.

THE WAY BACK

The return walk retraces the outward route, allowing you to enjoy an unbroken panorama over southern Lakeland. As height is lost, the surrounding peaks and lakes are gradually concealed one by one, as if sinking back into the earth from which they were revealed.

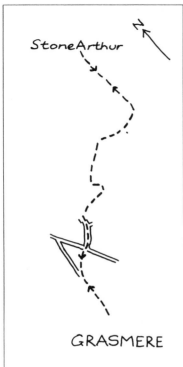

StoneArthur

GRASMERE

hearty early-morning meal before returning unmissed.

Chestnut trees
Not a native of Britain, the chestnut tree is thought to have been introduced by the Romans almost 2,000 years ago. It is no relation to the horse chestnut, whose fruits are avidly collected by children (young and old alike) and tempered to produce 'champions' in conker competitions. The sweet chestnut is in fact a member of the beech family, and its fruit was once a staple in the diet of peasants in parts of France. The nuts are delicious either roasted or boiled and are an essential ingredient in a wide range of winter dishes.

Sycamore trees
The sycamore is a member of the maple family, and is not native to this country. It is believed to have been introduced from central and southern Europe during medieval times. Its relative hardiness has enabled it to become well-established, but it is often disliked since its large, slowly decaying leaves smother the growth of woodland flowers.

ALONG THE WAY
Porridge
There is a tale that the novelist Walter Scott, when staying with the Wordsworths at Dove Cottage, became so fed up with their regular bland morning diet of porridge, that he took to climbing out of his bedroom window and visiting the Swan Inn for a

WALK 12
GRISEDALE TARN

*Grisedale Tarn is a small lake, lying at the head of a high valley behind
Seat Sandal and Fairfield to the north of Grasmere. Its waters flow
down to Patterdale and therefore one might argue a closer association
with Ullswater. Nevertheless, it can be conveniently reached from the
Rothay Valley and thus its inclusion in this collection of walks is
justified.*

Start/Finish: Grasmere. GR.336076.
Total distance: 13km (8 miles).
Height gain: 610m (1998 feet).
Difficulty: The long and steady climb into the mountains is generally
clear, but care is necessary in poor weather.

THE WALK

Rather than follow the main road
from Grasmere, leave the village along Easedale Road and,
immediately after crossing
Goody Bridge, turn right along
Underhelm. Go to the end of the
lane, turn right again and cross
Low Mill Bridge, walking up to
the main (A591) road.

Cross over and follow a track
opposite beside a row of cottages (marked to Patterdale).
Beyond a gate, carry on beside
Tongue Gill, the brook babbling
noisily as if celebrating its
release from the marshy mountain uplands. After a second
gate, walk by some drystone
sheep enclosures to the conflu-
ence of Little Tongue and

Tongue Gills, which are separated by the grassy sloping ridge
of Great Tongue.

A bridge or stepping stones
takes you across Little Tongue
Gill to a junction. Choose the
left-hand path, a distinct grass
track climbing beside the
stream. After levelling off it re-
crosses the gill and resumes its
ascent, heading towards Seat
Sandal. Eventually, the climb
lessens and the path grows less
distinct over grass.

Continue walking generally
ahead, but bear to the left, where
a stony track climbs left around
some crags ahead. After a short
pull, it turns right and a clear
track then runs more or less
level above the crags around

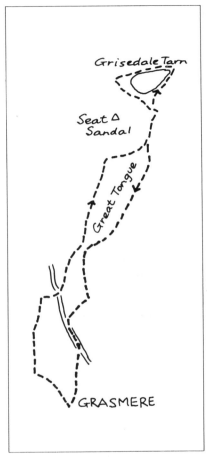

from the junction of the streams below.

Now a gently climbing path, it rises to a dry cwm, the amphitheatre contained by the steeply rising slopes of Seat Sandal on the left and Fairfield on the right. The path contours the flank of Seat Sandal before tackling a final steeper pull to Grisedale Hause, crossing a dry stone wall at the top between Seat Sandal and Fairfield. The way ahead is now clear, along a path around the right-hand side of Grisedale Tarn, dropping to the water at its north-eastern corner, where the tarn gives birth to Grisedale Beck.

THE WAY BACK

Cross the stream and walk around the lake's opposite bank, climbing at its western end to meet a path that has risen directly from Dunmail Raise. There, under the foot of Seat Sandal, turn left and return to Grisedale Hause.

At the Hause, turn right onto the path by which you came up, dropping first into the dry hollow and then on towards Tongue

the south-eastern slopes of Seat Sandal. After a while, at an unobtrusive cairn, it is joined by another path that has come up the other side of Tongue Gill

Gill. Just below the hollow, at the head of Tongue Gill, the path crosses a small stream and then forks beside a low cairn, you came up by the path on the right. However, now take the left fork, dropping to cross the infant Tongue Gill.

The path then moves left to leave the stream, which tumbles through a series of pretty cascades and clear pools, and there are fine views ahead as you make your descent into an ever- deepening valley.

Eventually, at a large boulder, the path splits, the main path branching right to meet Little Tongue Gill. However, keep ahead on a path that retains its height above the stream and shortly follows a wall. Pass through a succession of gates, in reality sheep pens, and keep going between stone walls to come to a gate on the right. Go through and drop across a rough sloping meadow, to join a track, the way being marked.

Follow the track to the left, leaving the meadow through a gate at its bottom left-hand corner into the next field. A waymark directs you beside the wall on the right to a gap, also waymarked. Turn right and walk to a barn, where a further waymark then directs you left to

a gate out of the field. A track past a cottage leads to the main (A591) road, some 200m/yds south of the Traveller's Rest Inn.

Turn left and then go right into Pye Lane. At the end, again go right to return to the centre of Grasmere.

ALONG THE WAY
Haematite
Haematite, an ore of iron and so called because of its red colour (the Greek 'haima' means blood), was found to outcrop around Great Tongue and two mines were started, Providence and Fairfield. In 1870, they were recorded as producing 500 tons of ore between, but poor prices for ore rendered them uneconomic and they were eventually closed.

Brothers' Parting
A short distance below Grisedale Tarn on the Patterdale side, to the right of the stream, is a boulder on which is carved Wordsworth's poem 'The Brothers' Parting'.

WALK 13
GIBSON KNOTT and HELM CRAG

Helm Crag stands sentinel at the head of Grasmere's flat-bottomed valley. It is the termination of a long ridge, which runs over Gibson Knott to the higher ground of Calf Crag and separates the valleys of Easedale and Greenburn. Its relatively diminutive size, when compared to the more massive bulks that lie around it, in no way detracts from the sense of achievement to be gained from its ascent or the magnificent panorama it offers from the top. An arduous direct ascent from Grasmere is avoided by a more gentle climb from Greenburn, joining the ridge for a fine walk over Gibson Knott to Helm Crag. Although the track from Greenburn Bottom is occasionally vague, it presents no navigational problems in good visibility.

Start/Finish: Grasmere. GR.336076.
Total distance: 11km (6¾ miles).
Height gain: 540m (1768 feet).
Difficulty: A long walk involving several climbs; take care in poor visibility, and near the crags on the ridge.

THE WALK

From Grasmere, walk along Easedale Road (signposted to Easedale Tarn), but just beyond Goody Bridge, turn right onto Underhelm, walking past Thorny How Youth Hostel and Underhelm Farm to a junction by Low Mill Bridge. Turn left to the cottages and farm at Ghyll Foot.

Where the lane then divides take the left fork, shortly reaching more cottages. At the end of the drive, beyond the second cottage, a gate opens to the National Trust land of Green Burn.

Walk ahead towards a stone wall, forking right on a clear track beside it up the valley. Beyond a gate, the track carries on, the wall now on the right and Green Burn below on the left. Higher up, beyond another gate, the bracken-covered fell rises on the right to Cotra Breast and the steep slopes of Gibson Knott rise beyond Greenburn on the left.

Eventually, the gradient eases and, although occasionally indistinct, the grassy path maintains its direction up the valley. You shortly reach the upper valley of Greenburn Bottom, a long amphitheatre steeply contained on three sides. Its entrance is closed by a lateral moraine, a mound of rocky debris left by the melting glacier that carved out the valley. Now grassed over, it is more suggestive of an Iron Age earthwork than a natural feature.

Beyond the moraine, bear left on an indistinct path to cross the emerging Green Burn by stepping stones. The path then leads half-right ahead, climbing gently up the valley side to pass the walled enclosure of an old sheep fold. Notice that its builders have incorporated the huge boulders within the wall where they lay rather than attempt to move them. A little further on, the path starts to lose height and you are brought to a low cairn, where a faint trod up the hillside leaves the main path.

Follow it, passing another cairn, to a third one, where the path then turns to the right, choosing an easier line of ascent. With the advantage of height, the valley's drainage pattern becomes clear. Small, slow flowing streams snake across the bottom, collecting water from the hillsides before combining at the eastern end into Green Burn.

The path then climbs more steeply, eventually turning to climb straight up the hillside. Low piles of stones mark the way to the top, a final one standing where it meets a clear path coming along the ridge from Calf Crag on the right. Turn left and follow the path over Gibson Knott and then down to Bracken Hause, from where the final pull to Helm Crag, which, although quite steep, is soon completed.

THE WAY BACK

Resume your way along the summit ridge, beyond 'the lion and the lamb', after which the path descends steeply over rocks to a grassy terrace. From there, a clear path drops to the right. It shortly turns left, between White Crag and Jackdaw Crag, eventually arriving at a wall.

Turn right down a steep path to reach some old quarries below Jackdaw Crag. The path then drops to the enclosing wall of a small plantation. Turn right beside the wall and then go left down a walled track, signposted to Grasmere.

Keep going through a gate and past some cottages to a

drive. Turn left and follow it past more cottages and then through a meadow to a gate. Ahead lies Easedale Road, which leads you back to Grasmere.

ALONG THE WAY

Behind Underhelm, Helm Crag rises steeply on the left and across on the other side of the valley, the massive bulk of Rydal Fell soars above lower tree lined slopes. Hard right is Heron Pike and, further north along the ridge, is Great Rigg. Ahead, Great Tongue drops steeply from Seat Sandal to the main road, which disappears at the top of the valley in search of Thirlmere and Keswick.

Greenburn's upper valley would at one time have held a tarn, and indeed today, remains marshy. Accumulations of organic matter from decaying plant life and drainage of the

47

lake's waters through the moraine have contributed to its present state. The eastern end of the valley floor is spotted with rounded hillocks, further accretions of the debris left behind by the retreating ice.

Butterwort

In places the ground is poorly drained, and different types of moss provide a spongy, if soggy carpet underfoot. Notice, hidden in the grass and moss of the wet patches, the shiny pale green leaves of the common butterwort or bog violet. In early summer, pretty violet pea-like flowers adorn the tops of single stalks, sprouting from the centre of the leafy base.

The plant is in fact carnivorous, supplementing the meagre supply of minerals that it gets from the acid peat in which it grows with nutrition from the bodies of insects who are unfortunate enough to alight upon the attractive looking leaves. When the insect lands, it is caught by a sticky secretion, and its struggle for freedom causes the leaf to curl around it. Once encased, the leaf releases enzymes, which effectively digest the still living prey, and the result is absorbed by the plant. Once the process

has been completed, the leaf opens again, and the remains of the insect are washed away in the next shower.

The name 'butterwort' may derive from the plant's traditional use in helping to curdle milk during the production of butter.

Helm Crag

Helm Crag's modest height is more than amply compensated for by the rugged nature of its top, far more worthy as a 'mountain summit' than those of many of the much loftier peaks around. The short ridge bristles with rocky outcrops that dramatically overhang a gully and crags on its north eastern face. The bare stone pinnacles stand out as clear silhouettes against the skyline as you approach, and the highest points can only be reached by a modest scramble, take care! Those with less of a head for heights will find that the views are equally rewarding from their bases. The northwesterly outcrop has been variously dubbed the 'lion couchant', 'old lady' or 'howitzer', whilst the south-easterly group portrays the famous 'lion and the lamb'.

WALK 14
FAR EASEDALE

*To the north-west of Grasmere, the long valley of Far Easedale
penetrates deeply into the high mountains. It offers an undemanding
but wonderfully satisfying walk into the heart of the hills.
The return is either by the outward route or, for the more energetic, a
climb up to Calf Crag before following the ridge over Gibson Knott and
Helm Crag.*

Start/Finish: Grasmere. GR.336076.
Total distance: 12km (7½ miles).
Height gain: 590m (1932 feet).
Difficulty: A linear walk; inexperienced walkers are advised not to
return along the Helm Crag ridge in poor visibility.

THE WALK

Leave the village along Easedale road, walking to its end, where a sign directs you onwards through a gate to Far Easedale. The metalled lane passes through a meadow, eventually ending at the gated entrance to Brimmer Head Farm. There, take a track on the right beside Easedale House and Jackdaw Cottage.

Walk ahead through a gate and turn left onto an enclosed track. Ignoring the sign on the right to Helm Crag a few m/yds on, and keep ahead towards Far Easedale and Borrowdale.

Eventually the valley begins to narrow and the path is brought to a springy wooden bridge across Far Easedale Gill.

Beyond, the valley briefly levels out and while the stream wanders aimlessly across its a shallow ill-drained floor, the path seeks the slightly higher and drier ground to the left. Ignore an obviously climbing path on the left, which passes beneath Stenners Crag and Cockly Crag to Easedale Tarn.

Beyond the bog, the valley again climbs to give a fine retrospective view past Helm Crag to Grasmere. Eventually, the upper valley comes into view ahead, the stream occasionally flecked white as its passage is broken by outcrops of rock. A

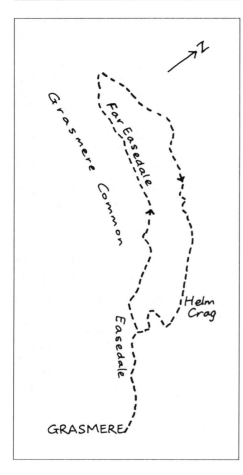

valley. At the top, the path levels to a rounded grassy col, an admirable spot with a wonderful sense of remoteness.

THE WAY BACK

If not retracing your steps, the route along the ridge is an enjoyable, if more strenuous, walk. There is no difficulty in clear weather, but in mist the path over Calf Crag is occasionally indistinct and care should be taken not to stray to the north.

Take a clear track on the right just before the crest of the coll. It maintains its height for a short distance, running back above the path by which you ascended. Shortly, it drops to cross a stream emanating

succession of alternating rises and marshy levels lead the path to a final determined pull, where it crosses the beck before ultimately climbing out of the

from a small tarn on the left, before then climbing to Calf Crag, the highest point of the ridge. Keep going, now gently losing height and bending around to the right on a winding path through grassy hillocks that avoids the worst of some boggy patches.

In clear weather, the way is obvious, but in mist, take care to stay with the line. The path soon becomes distinct again as it drops by Pike of Carrs. A prominent path now rises ahead over Gibson Knott and then falls to a saddle from which a short but steep pull climbs to Helm Crag.

Now downhill, the path leads to a grassy ledge at the end of the ridge. It then zigzags down, passing an abandoned quarry to reach the enclosing wall of wood at the foot of the fell.

Follow the wall to the right and then go left along a walled track. At the bottom, turn left to pass through a gate. Walk ahead, shortly joining Easedale Road back to Grasmere.

ALONG THE WAY

The hillside bracken indicates once fertile ground that would at one time have nourished a tree cover, predominantly of oak. Now, the few trees that remain are scattered, often beside the streams which course their way down to the beck. Others cling to inaccessible crags, where their first appearance as succulent seedlings is safeguarded from the unceasing nibbling of the sheep, who over the centuries have probably been the cause of as much deforestation as has man and his axe. The barer areas of marsh or coarse grass contain few nutrients and not many plants can survive in these places. The fertility of the soil has been leached away by streams or lost below layers of dead vegetation, deprived of oxygen to support the recycling processes.

Keep a look out for the large black dor beetles. They are commonly seen suicidally pottering amongst the stones on Lakeland paths, dodging the feet of passing walkers. They feed on dung, which they cache in underground tunnels to nourish their larvae. If you look at the underside of one, you will see that it has a beautiful iridescent blue-green colour.

WALK 15
EASEDALE TARN

It is a relatively easy walk from Grasmere to Easedale Tarn, a delightful little lake lying in a high valley. The path is steep for only one short section, but there are ample excuses to pause and savour the ever-changing retrospective view down the Rothay Valley as height is gained. The route is clear throughout and presents no navigational problems.

Start/Finish: Grasmere. GR.336076.
Total distance: 9km (5¾ miles).
Height gain: 230m (753 feet).
Difficulty: A popular walk; the way is clear, and presents no significant demands.

THE WALK

Walk from the centre of the village along Easedale Road, signposted to Easedale Tarn. Just before the end of the road, look for a signed footpath on the left over a bridge across Easedale Beck. Beyond, a wide track passes through two gates and crosses a slab bridge. After crossing meadows, the path begins climbing gently above a stream, Sourmilk Gill.

Seen ahead are waterfalls that give the stream its name, after heavy rain they are white from the foaming water cascading over the rocks. Further on, beyond another gate, the path climbs more purposefully to the top of the falls, carrying on beside a succession of connecting pools. Eventually, below Cockly Crag, the gradient eases and you are led below the steeply rising slopes that enclose Easedale Tarn.

THE WAY BACK

As an alternative to retracing your steps, a rewarding alternative lies around the lake, descending initially alongside Sourmilk Gill's opposite bank before crossing into the neighbouring valley of Far Easedale. A clear path follows the lake shore of the lake to its far end, and shortly after passing a lone holly tree, dips to a stream.

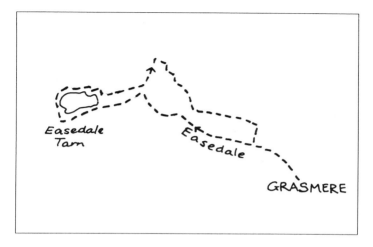

Leave the path there and follow the stream down to its junction with a second stream which can easily be crossed by stepping stones. Walk towards the lake and pick up a path around its far shore, which eventually returns you to Sourmilk Gill. At first, the continuing path runs beside the stream, but later moves away to the left.

A little distance further on, a waymark confirms the way to Grasmere and the path assumes a more deliberate descent into Far Easedale. The path eventually drops to Far Easedale Gill, joining a track coming from the head of the valley. Turn right and immediately cross the stream by a bridge to then follow a wide and sometimes rocky track to the foot of some quarries at Jackdaw Crag. Below the quarries, a walled track on the right, signposted 'Grasmere', leads through trees to a gate. Go through the gate and, as an alternative to returning via Easedale Road, immediately turn left through another gate, to follow a permissive footpath through Lancrigg Woods. The path is clear, and leads to a gap in a wall. Beyond, it winds through what was once a woodland garden, old walks twisting around the now unkempt trees, and dried-up ponds, the whole having an air of forgotten abandonment. Keep ahead along the main path to a fork, the right path leading directly to the garden of Lancrigg House, where teas are served in summer. The one to the left climbs to the crest of a small, wooded hill, where a modest plaque beside the path carries the legend:

HOC IN SUPERCILIO SEDEBAT DOROTHEA WORDSWORTH DUM EX ORE FRATRIS PROPE INAMBULANTIS CARMINA DESCRIBIT

which roughly translates as:

Dorothy Wordsworth used to sit at this spot, writing down the poems that her brother dictated as he walked nearby

Beyond, the track drops back through the trees, passing two successive gates into Lancrigg's garden. Walk past the house, leaving along its drive. Ignore the crossing track just beyond the cattle grid, and continue to the end to emerge at Easedale Road. Follow it back to Grasmere.

ALONG THE WAY
The Black Quarter
Although she often enjoyed walking in the Easedale valley, Dorothy Wordsworth referred to it as the 'Black Quarter', describing the sombre and melancholy appearance it adopts when heavy storm clouds gather. In those days, the cascades were known as Churn Milk Force, and she likened them "to a broad stream of snow".

The hanging valley, in which Easedale Tarn lies, has the appearance of a crater, enclosed by steep hillsides that rise on the right to Tarn Crag and on the left, Castle How and Blea Rigg. The lake fills the vast hollow, draining water from the surrounding hills and releasing it at its narrow mouth into Sourmilk Gill.

Around the lake lie grassy hillocks, piles of glacial debris left by the retreating ice as it melted some 20,000 years ago. Their slight elevation makes them ideal picnic spots from which to view the surrounding countryside.

Glacial action
It is interesting to compare the situation here with the valleys of Greenburn Bottom to the north or Blindtarn Moss to the south. All were similarly formed as a result of glacial action and,

as the waters melted, left with shallow lakes. However, accumulations of decaying vegetation have now displaced the tarns at Greenburn and Blindtarn, leaving a poorly drained peat bog whose acid soil is only tolerable to mosses and marsh plants.

Erratics

On the way down into Far Easedale, notice ahead to the right, two large and distinctive boulders, one rounded and the other flat-topped and from which a small tree sprouts. They are erratics, caught up by moving glacial ice and abandoned here as it melted. Also of interest is the pattern of walls on the opposite side of Easedale valley, enclosing small fields.

Enclosures

The process of land enclosure in the Lake District started early, in some places during Viking times. Walls continued to be built throughout the Middle Ages to act as boundaries delineating estates and separating high pastures. However, the majority of what we see today is more recent, and was prompted by land improvement and the enclosure of common grazing which took place in the 18th and 19th centuries. Because of the simplicity of the materials and construction method it is difficult to date any particular wall. Some clues can be gained from examining their structure. Those of the latter period can sometimes be recognised by 'hogg-holes', low openings in the wall which were either closed off or left open to control the movement of sheep between enclosures. The high labour cost of this traditional method of construction means that few such walls are being built today, and many repairs are neglected, the much cheaper but less aesthetic post and wire fence replacing them.

Lancrigg

With its fine, locally-styled chimneys, Lancrigg, was once the home of Sir John Richardson. Although by profession, he was a navy surgeon, he was also an accomplished naturalist and explorer, and took part in several Arctic expeditions. He also voyaged in the southern oceans and produced several studies on the animal and fish life that abounds in them. Born in Dumfries in 1787, his body lies in the churchyard at Grasmere, close to its entrance beside the gingerbread shop. The house is now a hotel.

WALK 16
SWINESCAR PIKE and LANG HOW

*Blind Tarn occupies a high valley above Easedale. Its name is
descriptive as the tarn that once occupied its shallow depression has
become a bog, but nonetheless, it is an attractive spot, and provides a
useful way up to the ridge behind. The climb up is a little strenuous,
but not difficult, and is followed by an easy walk along the broad ridge
before a gentle descent by way of Wray Gill to Allan Bank, one of the
houses occupied for a time by Wordsworth.*

Start/Finish: Grasmere. GR.336076.
Total distance: 7km (4½ miles).
Height gain: 350m (1146 feet).
Difficulty: The climb to Swinescar is long and in places steep. Caution
should be exercised in poor weather.

THE WALK

Follow Easedale road out of
Grasmere, walking almost to its
end to leave by a path through
the wall on the left across
Easedale Beck.

Keep going, through a gate
and along a wide, roughly paved
track. Shortly, the stream, having moved away from the path,
returns. Just beyond that point,
go through a wooden field-gate
in the wall on the left, crossing
the meadow to another gate at
its far right-hand corner. This
leads into a small enclosed
wood, where a track runs ahead
beside the right-hand boundary
wall. Follow this, leaving by

another gate and keep going to
a cottage and outbuildings at
the far side of a meadow.

Walk past the buildings and
through a wooden field-gate
onto the open fellside and follow a wall on the left to cross a
small stream.

Turn left and climb beside the
stream to another wall, where a
waymark directs you right on a
clear rising path above the
steep-sided gorge of Blindtarn
Gill. Above the top of the waterfall, the path levels to work its
way more easily around the left
edge of Blindtarn Moss, heading towards a gully in the far
hillside, Swinescar Hause.

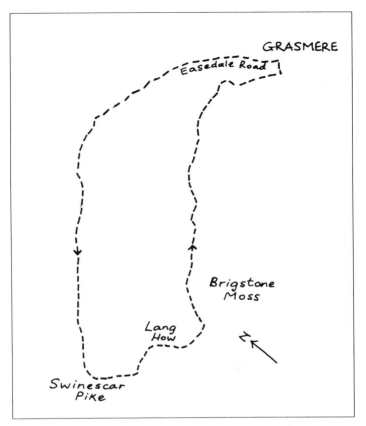

The path climbs quite steeply away from the moss and, although it occasionally becomes indistinct, the way is never in doubt. There are occasional cairns to guide you generally ahead until the path eventually runs beside the stream.

Ultimately, the path levels out onto grass, rising gently to the head of the gully where it meets a distinct path from Great Castle How on the right. Turn left and pass around the far side of the low summit of Swinescar Pike which lies above you to the left.

It is worth a short detour to its top for the view back into Easedale and of the surrounding hills. To the south-west lies the Langdale valley, and the hill opposite is Lingmoor Fell. Further right lie Pike of Blisco, Crinkle Crags and Bow Fell. Behind in the far distance, you might see Scafell.

Return to the path and follow its winding way across the hillocky topography. Shortly a small tarn comes into view. The main path bends to pass it on the left, Lang How rising now above you. Although there is no obvious path to its top, there is no difficulty in ascending the grassy bank to the high point.

THE WAY BACK

Return to the path by the tarn and resume your former direction. After shortly passing a smaller tarn, the path divides at a cairn, the more obvious left-hand fork dropping below the craggy easterly aspect of Lang How. Beyond another little tarn, the path again divides at a low cairn and, as before, select the left-hand path, continuing below Lang How. The path gently winds downwards, eventually running for a short distance beside a gully on the right containing Wray Gill.

Shortly, it then moves left through copses of juniper before dropping steeply by another stream, this time on the left. Beyond the juniper, continue downwards to the corner of a stone wall.

Ignore the path going right, but keep going with the wall on your right to reach a gate. Once through, walk down a walled track, which eventually opens up on the left and leads to another gate. Ahead, after passing a barn and cottage on your left, go through another gate and finally join a lane. Turn right and follow it past Allan Bank. At the end, over a cattle grid, it becomes Tannercroft, and leads back into Grasmere.

ALONG THE WAY
Blindtarn Gill

From the head of Blindtarn Gill, there is a fine view to the right of a waterfall, which after heavy rain, is a most impressive sight. The shelter provided by the acclivitous valley sides has allowed trees to become established and a surprising number and variety crowd its narrow ledges, oak, holly, rowan and birch being easily identified amongst them. Growing in profusion around the waterfall is juniper, its dark green foliage of needles being attractive at any time of year.

Juniper

Juniper, or savin, is one of only three conifers native to Britain, the other two being yew and Scots pine. In sheltered conditions, it can achieve the proportions of a small tree. On the open fell, however, it tends to produce low thickets, as here on the slopes around Blindtarn. The branches grow in grotesque shapes and are clothed in prickly needles and small berries, which are in fact cones. These are used as a spice and give gin its distinctive flavour. Juniper was once commercially grown, its wood producing a high quality charcoal, a component in the manufacture of gunpowder. There were several factories in the area producing 'black powder' from the mid-18th century onwards, one being located not far away at Elterwater.

Yew

Yew also grows hereabouts, occasionally seen on the fellside but more predictably in many of the small churchyards in the area. Various reasons are given to account for this association, one being that they mark pagan ritual sites, another that the trees sheltered early Christian missionaries and a third to ensure a ready source of wood from which to manufacture the traditional long-bow. The seeds of its attractive red berries are very poisonous.

Blindtarn Moss

In antiquity, Blindtarn Moss, the vast hollow scooped out of the mountainside by an ancient glacier, would have contained a tarn. It has long since disappeared, leaving a spacious empty amphitheatre. Its flat base is clothed in marshy vegetation, and drained by streams that gradually assert themselves as they approach the lip of the valley to emerge as Blind Tarn Gill. Around its perimeter, the rising hillsides are dotted with thickets of juniper bush, which on a hot dry day, give the place an almost Mediterranean feel.

WALK 17
SILVER HOW and DOW BANK

To the north-west of Grasmere, behind Grasmere Common, stands High Raise. From it runs a long ridge that separates Langdale and Elterwater from the Rothay valley. The ridge terminates above Ambleside in the extremities of Loughrigg Fell. This walk explores a section of that ridge above Grasmere, where arguably, it is at its most picturesque.

Start/Finish: Grasmere. GR.336076.
Total distance: 8.5km (5¼ miles).
Height gain: 470m (1539 feet).
Difficulty: Most of the ascent comes in the early part of the walk; take care in poor visibility.

THE WALK

Easedale Road leads the walk out of Grasmere, but just before the Glen Thorne Quaker Guest House, go through an iron gate in the wall into a field on the left. It is signed 'Score Crag and Langdale'.

Cross the field, making for a large cream-coloured house, Allan Bank, at its far side. A spring, rising in the middle of the field and creating a rather wet patch, can be avoided by passing on the right. Before reaching the house, turn right onto a tarmac drive and follow it upwards.

At a fork, bear left to Silver How and Langdale and walk on, passing some houses on your right, to a kissing-gate. Then, follow a rising grass track with a wall on the left. It shortly becomes stony and then enclosed on both sides. After a while, the gradient eases, and you pass through a kissing-gate onto the open fell.

A clear path ahead initially retains the left-hand wall for company, and although the way is inclined to be wet, stepping stones have been thoughtfully provided at the worst spots.

As the wall later curves away, remain with the grass track, climbing the hillside to a stone wall. The path there turns right, continuing its climb through a grove of juniper bushes and then above a shallow gully,

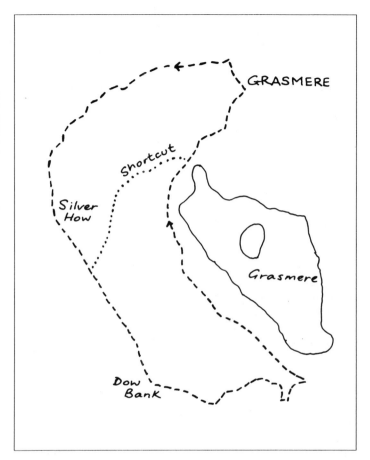

whose bracken covered slopes fall to the right.

The ascending path is occasionally cairned and later levels off to reach a fork. Take the left branch, which leads above another gully, this time on the left, its steep sides containing the lively stream of Wray Gill.

Follow the gill for a short distance and, where the path again divides, drop into the gully to cross the stream. A grass path then climbs to pass a rocky outcrop on the right.

The onward path is clear, Silver How now rising directly ahead. After levelling to cross one of the boggy areas which feed Wray Gill (in wet weather the worst of the marsh can be avoided by detouring slightly to the right), walk towards the foot of Silver Howe, where the path crosses a small stream emanating from a shallow gully. A final climb takes you to the top.

From this aspect, the summit is certainly not impressive, asserting itself little more than the neighbouring humps that rise from the grassy plateau. However, from the east, as you will see on the way down, it assumes a more spectacular profile. Steep crags overlook the western end of Grasmere and provide a superb viewpoint on a clear day. The grassy hollows surrounding the top provide perfect places in which to enjoy your picnic.

THE WAY BACK

Continue across the summit, resisting the temptation to deviate to the right.

After a few m/yds a grass path drops down, curving gently to the left and heading directly towards the conspicuous quarries above Elter Water in the distance. The way traverses a slope overlooking Grasmere and then crosses a number of streams before finally arriving at a large cairn. The path now drops steeply to the left, picking its way through some rocks. Little legs will find this short stretch more of a scramble, but there is no problem in its negotiation.

The path then runs out onto a broad grass and bracken-covered saddle where there is a crossing of routes.

ALTERNATIVE RETURN

For a shorter return to Grasmere, turn left and follow a path below the foot of Silver How. After crossing a stream, pass by a small ruined building on the left. The substantial ironmongery that litters the site is indicative of mining operations, although it has been described as a shooting hut.

Beyond, gently drop across a sloping hillside to reach a wall and keep going ahead, eventually coming to a kissing-gate.

Cross the sloping pasture beyond to another kissing gate at the bottom from which an enclosed track leads to a gate beside Kelbarrow on Red Bank Road.

Turn left and walk back to Grasmere.

TO CONTINUE

Otherwise keep ahead, the path passing to the left of the top of Spedding Crag and dropping beyond it to another shallow saddle. Climb ahead up the other side to the top of Dow Bank. On the other side, the path falls steeply to a large cairn and divides. Take the left fork, the path dropping to cross a marshy area towards a small grassy pond.

Before reaching the pond, fork left and climb to a rocky top, beyond which, you reach the corner of a stone wall. Walk on beside a descending wall to the bottom of another dip and again, climb up the far side by a wall to a fence and go through a kissing-gate. Keep going, still with the wall on your left, but now dropping. The path shortly leaves the wall and falls beside a plantation of larch finally to meet a road. Turn right and then, almost immediately, left onto a bridleway into Deer Bolts Wood.

A short distance down, at a gate, go left through a kissing-gate onto a woodland path above Grasmere. The track traverses a steeply-sloping wooded hillside, ending by a cottage on Red Bank Road. Turn right to return to Grasmere.

ALONG THE WAY
Allan Bank

Allan Bank was built in 1805 by a Liverpool business man, Mr Crump. By all accounts it was badly designed and had a reputation for being damp and having smoking chimneys and draughty passages. Wordsworth rented it for three years, appreciating the space after the small confines of Dove Cottage, but was not sorry when his lease ended.